Elizabeth Fry

Terry Barber

ACTIVIST
SERIES

Elizabeth Fry is published by
Grass Roots Press, a division of Literacy Services of Canada Ltd.

www.grassrootsbooks.net

ACKNOWLEDGMENTS

We acknowledge the financial support of the Government of Canada through the Canada Book Fund (CBF) for our publishing activities.

Produced with the assistance of
the Government of Alberta, Alberta
Multimedia Development Fund.

Alberta
Government

Editor: Dr. Pat Campbell
Image research: Dr. Pat Campbell
Book design: Lara Minja, Lime Design Inc.

Library and Archives Canada Cataloguing in Publication

Barber, Terry, date
    Elizabeth Fry / Terry Barber.

ISBN 978-1-894593-89-2

    1. Fry, Elizabeth Gurney, 1780-1845. 2. Prison reformers—Great Britain—Biography. 3. Quakers—Great Britain—Biography. 4. Readers for new literates. I. Title.

PE1126.N43B36335 2008   428.6'2   C2008-901999-7

Contents

A British prisoner.

Prison Life

It is the early 1800s. The prisons in Britain are **hellholes**. Men, women, and children are put in prisons. The prisons are smelly and dirty. Rats run across the floor. People sleep on the cold, dirty floor.

At Newgate Prison, 300 women and children share two rooms.

Prisoners walk in a circle for exercise.

The exercise yard at Newgate Prison.

Prison Life

The prisons are crowded. Killers and thieves share the same space. People cook, eat, and sleep in the same space. People go to the bathroom in the same space. People get sick from the living conditions. Many people die in prison.

A man is hanged in England, 1824.

Prison Life

British laws are harsh. People are hanged for small crimes. People are hanged for stealing clothes. People are hanged for cutting down a tree. People can be hanged for over 200 crimes. People **rot** in prison for small crimes.

Women beg for milk in a prison.

Prison Life

The women and children are hungry.
They need money to buy food. They
have no money. They fight with one
another for money. Women beg for
food. In prison, time is long and hope
is short.

Each
prisoner gets
2 lbs. of meat and
1 lb. of bread
a week.

Elizabeth in 1818.

Prison Life

The women and children need
support. But nobody wants to help
them. In 1813, a young mother
decides to help. Her name is Elizabeth
Fry. She will make life better for
women and children in prison.

The home of Elizabeth and her family.

Early Years

Elizabeth is born in 1780. She is born into a rich family. Her father is a banker. Her parents are Quakers. Most Quakers speak and dress in a plain way. Elizabeth's family is different. The women wear silk gowns.

Quakers are members of the Religious Society of Friends.

Quakers give soup to poor people.

Early Years

Quakers believe that all people are children of God. They believe that all people are equal. They believe that men and women are equal. This is not a common belief in the 1700s. Quakers work for social justice.

The Quaker way of life is simple.

Elizabeth Fry's sewing basket.

Early Years

In the 1700s, most girls do not get a good education. Elizabeth's mother believes girls need a good education. Elizabeth learns how to sew. She also learns the same subjects as boys. She learns how to speak French and Latin.

Elizabeth also learns about history and geography.

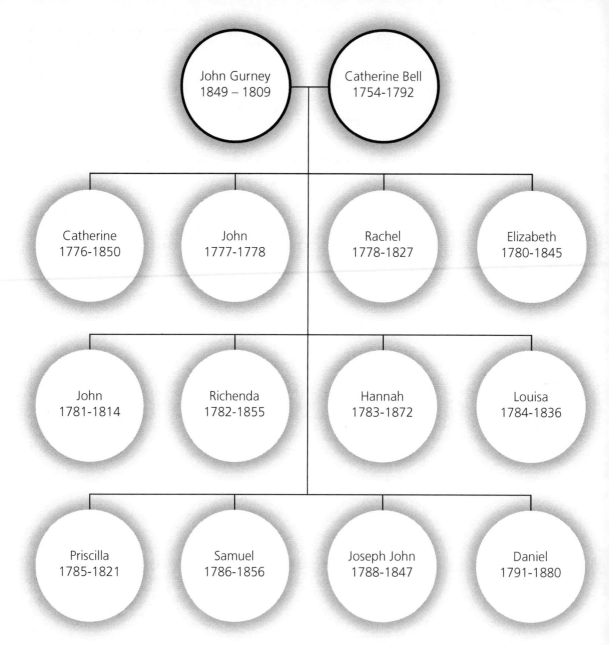

Family Tree

Early Years

Elizabeth also learns to care for others. When Elizabeth is 12, her mother dies. Elizabeth has eight younger brothers and sisters. She helps to raise the younger children. Elizabeth knows how to care for her brothers and sisters.

A Quaker woman preaches.

Early Years

Elizabeth meets a preacher when she is 18. The preacher predicts Elizabeth's future. Elizabeth will become "a light to the blind." Elizabeth will become "feet to the **lame**." Elizabeth takes these words to heart. She wants to help others lead better lives.

Elizabeth, age 19.

A Quaker marriage.

Wife and Mother

A rich man falls in love with Elizabeth.
He asks, "Will you marry me?"
Elizabeth says, "No." She thinks the
man is **dull**. Elizabeth gets to know
him better. She grows to love him.
His name is Joseph Fry. Elizabeth
agrees to marry him.

Elizabeth
and Joseph
marry in 1800.

A family in 1801.

Wife and Mother

Most husbands think their wives should stay at home. Women should raise the children. Women should cook, clean, and wash clothes. Women should take care of their husbands. Joseph is different. He supports Elizabeth's work outside the home.

Joseph Fry in 1823.

By 1830, only seven children live at home.

Joseph and Elizabeth Fry's children.

Wife and Mother

Elizabeth's first child is born in 1801. She has 11 more children. But Elizabeth is lucky. She has servants to help her. Elizabeth is able to work outside the home. In 1813, Elizabeth visits a prison.

Elizabeth has 12 children in 20 years.

Women and children suffer at Newgate Prison.

Elizabeth Visits Prisons

Prison life shocks Elizabeth. She sees a dead baby lying on the cold floor. She sees two women taking off the baby's clothes. They need the clothes for another child. Elizabeth's heart melts. She has to help these women and children.

Elizabeth visits Newgate Prison.

31

Elizabeth and a friend visit Newgate Prison.

Elizabeth Visits Prisons

Elizabeth and other women make warm clothes for the babies. Elizabeth returns to the prison with a friend. They bring clothes for the babies. They bring fresh straw for bedding. Elizabeth brings a Bible. She prays with the women.

Elizabeth makes three visits to Newgate Prison in 1813.

War of 1812 battle.

Hard Times

The War of 1812 is bad for business
in England. By 1813, Joseph's business
is in trouble. The Frys must move to a
smaller home. The Fry's four-year old
child dies. Elizabeth does not visit a
prison for four years.

The
War of 1812
lasts three years.

Elizabeth starts a school for the children.

Prison Reform

It is 1816. Elizabeth and other women return to the prison. They start a school for the children. They teach the prisoners to read and sew. The prisoners sell the things they sew. They use the money to buy food and clothes.

Elizabeth reads to the prisoners.

Prison Reform

Elizabeth wants to **reform** the prison system. Elizabeth and her friends talk to the prisoners. They make a list of reforms. These reforms bring peace into the prison. These reforms bring hope into the prison.

One of the reforms is that prisons must educate prisoners.

Two closed wagons sit in front of Newgate Prison.

Prison Reform

England sends many prisoners to
Australia by ship. The prisoners
travel to the ships in open wagons.
Crowds throw stones and yell at the
prisoners. Elizabeth wants to protect
the prisoners. She tells the prison to
use closed wagons.

This ship takes
prisoners to
Australia.

This map shows the Elizabeth Fry societies in Canada.

A Role Model

For the rest of her life, Elizabeth
helps others. She gets other women
to help the poor. She starts a school
for nurses. Women in other countries
learn about Elizabeth's work. These
women form groups to help others.

There
are 26
Elizabeth Fry
societies in
Canada.

Elizabeth Fry in 1843.

A Role Model

Elizabeth Fry does more than help prisoners. She does more than help the poor. Elizabeth is a role model. Women begin to see they have lives outside the home. Elizabeth helps to free women to lead more useful lives.

Elizabeth Fry dies from a stroke in 1845.

JOSEPH FRY
DIED 1861
AGED 84
ELIZABETH, WIFE OF
JOSEPH FRY
DIED 1845
AGED 65

Glossary

dull: not interesting.

hellhole: a place of extreme misery.

lame: disabled in the leg or foot.

reform: to change something and make it better.

rot: to decay.

Talking About the Book

What did you learn about Elizabeth Fry?

What did you learn about Quakers?

Compare prison life in the 1800s to prison life in the 21 century.

Do you think Elizabeth Fry was a feminist? Why or why not?

How did Elizabeth Fry make the world a better place?

Picture Credits

Made in the USA
Monee, IL
21 February 2025

12329356R00032